Higher Education and Eco

Yian Chen

Higher Education and Economic Progress: The Case of BRICS Economies

Interactive Dynamics between Tertiary Education and Economic Expansion

LAP LAMBERT Academic Publishing

Cover image: www.ingimage.com

Publisher:
LAP LAMBERT Academic Publishing
is a trademark of
International Book Market Service Ltd., member of OmniScriptum Publishing Group
17 Meldrum Street, Beau Bassin 71504, Mauritius

Printed at: see last page
ISBN: 978-613-9-45725-0

Zugl. / Approved by: Suzhou, Xi'an Jiaotong-Liverpool University, 2019

TABLE OF CONTENT

1. Introduction

The term BRIC was firstly put forward by O'Neill (2001) in a research paper of Goldman Sachs that referred specifically to the Russian Federation, Federative Republic of Brazil, Republic of India, and the People's Republic of China as being at a comparable stage of socioeconomic development. A global economic power shift in the direction of these emerging markets was found and it had already been taking place as the potential of this bloc grew smoothly and steadily and it was also anticipated to outshine the G7 league by the end of 2027 (Foroohar, 2009). At the end of 2010, the inclusion of the Republic of South Africa changed the name to "BRICS". The member countries thereby collaborate on the principle of non-interference and equality that looks for the maximum multilateral benefit, while they also aim to counterbalance the occidental longstanding hard power by smoothly transforming their economic force into stronger political influence (Lopes, 2015). Numerically speaking, BRICS nations span across 4 continents, take up 26% of land mass worldwide, represent approximately 50% of the entire global population and produce a nominal gross domestic product of 16.6 trillion US dollars in total, which is equivalent to around a quarter of the global output (Smialek, 2015). The*2016-2017 Global Competitiveness Report* has produced a list of ranking of countries based on twelve different indicators, it was found that the average ranking of BRICS outweighs the global average performance; in terms of the market size, efficiency of labor market as well as the macroeconomic environment, the average ranking of BRICS countries is even higher than the OECD's average figure. In addition, the health index of BRICS has been increasing; the gap in primary education and tertiary education between the BRICS and the more advanced OECD group has been reduced smoothly due to the growing investment in personnel training by BRICS (Schwab, 2016). The progress BRICS nations have made in promoting economic development so far can be chiefly credited to the abundance of natural resources, a plethora of foreign direct investment as well as the comparatively cheap labor force; however, Zhong (2012) pointed out that in the current knowledge-based economy, research & development and innovation play a critical role in a country's sustainable development, thereupon tertiary education institutions and scientific research centers should be paid a higher degree of attention to. Global economic boom commencing in the 1960s was first and foremost based on significant technology advancement for example in the field of electronics and petrochemicals, thus leading to the development of tertiary education with particular emphasis on science and technology subjects. The gross enrollment rate of tertiary education in the United States reached 80.6% in 1996, and meanwhile the similar trend can be observed in Japan and Western Europe, where the gross tertiary education enrollment rate increased significantly in decades (Carnoy, Loyalka and Froumin, 2013). Along with economic progress made by the BRICS countries, the growth in the education sector also became prominent. In sharp contrast to the single-digit university enrollment rate in China in the decade before the millennium, this figure increased dramatically to 23% in 2007 with 70 million tertiary graduates and it was ranked second worldwide as in terms of the number of workers having at least a bachelor's degree (Ying, 2008, p.86). In addition, India has more than 420 higher education institutions with more

2

than 11 million students enrolling in colleges annually (Beddie, 2009). Tertiary education institutions have been growing at a rapid pace in Russia with over 6 million students enrolled in more than 1,200 universities (Ardichvili, Zavyalova and Minina, 2012). The expansion of tertiary education institutions and students were growing at 12% and 11% respectively in Brazil ever since the new millennium, reaching two thousand universities and colleges as well as four million registered students in the past ten years (Kosack, 2009). Transformation in the higher education sector in South Africa over the past twenty years has been characterized by a series of post-apartheid reforms that strive to reduce educational inequality by developing a more balanced and coherent system that could offer higher education to both white, colored and black citizens (Boughey and McKenna, 2011). In recent time, the South African higher education enrollment was 15.4% and it has been increasing at an annual average rate of 6.2% with Africans accounting for around two-thirds of the student population, which was more than twice the ratio compared with the level in the beginning of 1990 (Badsha and Nico, 2011). Early research has established a positive relationship between investment in higher education and economic expansion in which the education sector contributes significantly to both individual and societal advancement (Schultz, 1961a; Becker, 1978). Human resource development by way of mass education, in particular at the tertiary level, improves productivity on the organizational level and is deemed the only way that leads to industrial upgrading and economic structural transformation (Lynham and Cunningham, 2006). The rise of the BRICS countries can therefore be associated to the advancement of their tertiary educational level.

3

2. Literature Review

The aim of the literature review is to identify pieces of theoretical foundation in academia that relates to the analysis of human capital development, higher education structure and economic advancement as well as the interactions between them. Samuelson (1948) regarded increased economic output as an outward shift of the curve of production possibility frontier, suggesting that a country's output and services have been constantly growing, which was because of an increase in the resources and efficiency. Nevertheless, Lewis (1955) argued that economic growth was not only deemed the growth in output, but should also be the sustainable growth of the per capita value of output. Kuznets (1971) advanced another theory that includes two additional factors to consider: the increasing supply of goods and services epitomizes economic advancement; institutional innovation and technological progress are the necessary and sufficient condition for economic development. The relationship between education and growth of economic output has been investigated extensively thanks to the growing interest in the sources of economic growth and a stronger importance of tertiary education. In the field of Classical Economics, as predominantly represented by Adam Smith, capital accumulation was often deemed the sole determinant of economic growth. Neoclassical economics, for example the Solow model, advanced the previous assumption by taking into account of labor and capital as the endogenous factors and technology the exogenous factor that materialize growth. It was not until the endogenous growth theory, which assumed that labor specialization and human capital development determined the level of endogenous technological innovation, went popular that the role of tertiary education was widely explored (Hult, 2009). Schultz's (1960) theory of human capital stated that human resource development by means of investment in education contributed to economic expansion in a similar pattern as accumulation of capital. It was later discovered that the average rate of return to educational investment in the United States between 1929 and 1957 was 17%, and the contribution rate from higher education was approximately 32.49% (Schultz, 1961b; Denison, 1985). Maddison (1992) calibrated the effect of expanding tertiary education to economic growth in the Western economies after World War I, and found that the contribution became considerably higher after 1970s. Romer (1986), Lucas (1988) and Barro (1990)'s revolutionary research indicated that tertiary education was not an exogenous variable but an endogenous impetus that leads to positive externality. There was a U-shaped relationship between the years of schooling and increased economic output and the optimum length of schooling was found to be seven and a half years, above which point the positive impact could be gradually offset (Freeman, 1976; Autor, Katz and Krueger, 1998). Meanwhile, other scholars also examined the dynamics of this relationship and arrived at varied conclusions. By making use of a quantitative approach, Menon (1997) concluded that education caused economic advancement while Card (1999) arrived at an opposite statistically causal relationship. Goetz and Rupasingha (2003) investigated the return of higher education with cross-sectional datasets in various states in America and indicated that different socioeconomic stages of development benefited from higher education in dissimilar fashions, the higher the better and more effective. Ma and Mao (2004) used empirical evidence to demonstrate that there was a short term dynamic and long term equilibrium status in which economic expansion advances higher educational development. Fan (2006, p.120) further argued that economic development increases demand for higher education, and subsequently higher education raises labor productivity, thus the well educated human capital provides favorable response to the economy. Zhao, Yu and Liu (2011) used co-integration and impulse response function instruments to analyze the dynamics between higher educational input and growth in the economy and came to the conclusion that GDP would grow by 0.3% and 1.2% respectively with an additional 1% investment in funding and human resources in tertiary education. The economic development of a country relies on human capital through the improvement of education level; investment in tertiary education was to ensure a sustainable increase in productivity and efficiency of the human factor (McConnell and Brue, 1988, p.77) Nafukho, Hairston and Brooks (2004) argued that human capital can also be evaluated by the level of education, and educational structure could imply the demand for skills in the economy. The structure of higher education largely referred to the layer structure and it reflected every hierarchy's combination and interrelation. Generally speaking, tertiary educational structure includes vocational training, undergraduate and postgraduate academic study (Hao and Wang, 1987). Increase in GDP was also differently affected by factors such as the number of ordinary graduates from higher education, workers from vocational training schools and scholars and professors from research institutions. Thereupon, the employed civilian population would exert different levels of impact to the economy, suggesting a role the educational structure could play in GDP growth (Zaharia, Popescu and Feniser, 2016). Empirical investigations about catalysts for the success of the Asian Four Tigers (South Korea, Singapore, Hong Kong and Taiwan) demonstrated that continuous adjustment of educational structure was an important practice with direct effects (Gao, 1998). A large portion of existing empirical literature devoted to examining such connection between tertiary education and economic advancement for an individual country or at most for members of regional blocs. Nonetheless, there is a scarcity of studies that compare this relationship among the BRICS countries. Hence, this project intends to fill this gap to include individual analysis of this "higher education — economic expansion" interaction from the perspective of size and structure in Russia, Brazil, India, China and South Africa respectively as well as to put it in a more holistic framework so that a comparative study can be accomplished.

3. Research Questions and Objectives

Existing research framework has been focusing on the effect that higher education brings to the national economic growth by implementing a holistic approach to the variables of funding and size. This project aims to extend the framework by looking into the dynamic interaction between tertiary educational size and BRICS economic expansion as well as the impact the tertiary education structure brings to the individual BRICS economy. Based on the academic theories complied in the literature review section, it is hypothesized that the enrollment of tertiary education

7

will not only be statistically caused by changes in the national economy but will also statistically influence the national economic performance, i.e. an interactive causality relationship exists between them. It is also projected that academic training at the tertiary level would make more contribution to the economic advancement than the tertiary vocational education does. Since the variables of this project are country-level indices related to tertiary education and economic status, I would structure my analysis based on the macro data and rely upon the basic econometric knowledge to evaluate. Another objective of this study is to present a comparative analysis of the tertiary education sector across the BRICS nations from different perspectives that can reflect educational progress achieved by the respective countries and to pave the way for follow-up research.

4. Methodology

This study is based upon the secondary data and the interaction between the higher education enrollment and economic expansion for each and every BRICS country will be investigated. The relevant indicators for the BRICS were collected from official websites of international organizations and they have a time span of 21 years starting from 1994 and ending in 2014. For simplification purposes, the population of total enrollment (EDU)can be used to indicate the size of higher education, and employ gross domestic product (GDP) as an index to evaluate economic growth. GDP figures for all BRICS countries were extracted from the World Bank national accounts. The gross enrollment population for each BRICS country was found on the

UNESCO Institute for Statistics, and the value of which was calculated by multiplying the total population of the age group who are within five years after leaving secondary school by the gross enrollment ratio at the tertiary level. The GDP value of each country was then converted to the real term by using the 2010 official exchange rates to US dollars. In the next step, logarithm of both EDU and GDP was taken to eliminate heteroscedasticity and denote them as LEDU and LGDP respectively. Nevertheless, in reality time series data often change without any statistical law and thus the randomness could renders the series non-stationary where an impact effect is non-negligibly longstanding; thus they could produce a "spurious regression" output, which fails to reflect the actual statistical trend. In this case, the co-integration analysis overcomes this weakness and it would be more reliable to find out the interaction between two or more time series. In this project, Augmented Dickey Fuller (ADF) Test will be firstly used to assess stationarity. If the null hypothesis of a unit root is rejected, then the time series is stationary and the conventional regression analysis can be proceeded with. If however the test result turns out to be insignificant, then the original time series is non-stationary and a first difference of the variable should be exercised to assess if it could reach stationarity afterwards. If the two time series are both found to be integrated of order one, then it can be presumed that a co-integration relationship may exist between these time series. When involving no more than two variables, the Engle—Granger Test will be executed to determine the existence of the co-integration relationship, which implies a long-term equilibrium status and thus a statistically significant causal relationship. The next step will be to find out the direction of the statistical causality, I will base my analysis on the Granger Causality Test to evaluate the dynamics. If a variable is found to be significantly helpful to predict changes of another variable, then adding additional past values of the first variable could strengthen the regression effect, suggesting that the first variable Granger Causes the second variable. The optimal number of lags will be selected based upon the BIC (Schwarz) criterion. The above three tests will be performed one after another for each BRICS country followed by a comparative analysis of the statistical output. With regard to the second research question, the traditional linear regression model can be computed to measure the impact of different higher education levels to the economic growth. The structure of tertiary education will be differentiated by the population of students enrolled in the vocational training colleges (VOE) and those enrolled in bachelor's degree programs as well as in Master's or PhD degree programs (EDU). Likewise, logarithm of these variables will be calculated to remove heteroscedasticity and will be denoted as LGDP, LVOE and LEDU. A conventional regression for each BRICS country can be running over the period of 21 years with LGDP being the dependent variable and LVOE and LEDU being the independent variables. After assessing the significance of the independent variables, the magnitude of each independent variable will be employed to compare the level of contribution of each layer within the higher educational framework to the respective economic expansion in each country. The first part of the analysis will chiefly be based on the statistical package Eviews 6.0 and the second section related to the multi-variable linear regression model will be performed by Stata13.0.

5. Models and Findings

a. Research Question 1

With regard to the first research question, this project opted for the number of total enrollment and a standardized comparable GDP parameter to indicate higher educational size and economic development respectively. After taking logarithm for both types of statistics, I use Microsoft Excel to demonstrate the time trend of the time series for five different BRICS countries. Figure 1 below is shown as follows:

Time Trend of Russia's LEDU and LGDP (1994-2014)

Value in log term

RUS_LEDU
RUS_LGDP

Time Trend of Brazil's LEDU and LGDP (1994-2014)

Value in log term

— BRA_LEDU
— BRA_LGDP

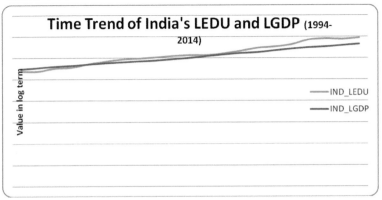

Time Trend of India's LEDU and LGDP (1994-2014)

Value in log term

— IND_LEDU
— IND_LGDP

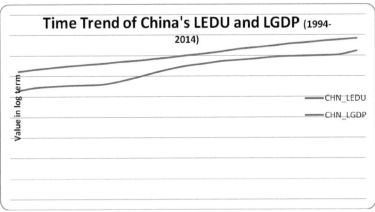

Time Trend of China's LEDU and LGDP (1994-2014)

Value in log term

— CHN_LEDU
— CHN_LGDP

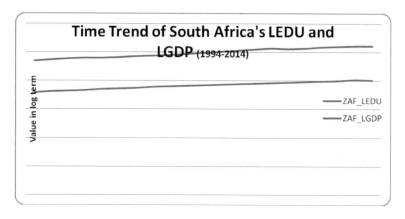

Figure 1: Time trends for BRICS.

The overall trend is that the values are growing within the time frame, however times series in many cases are not stationary. If a regression analysis is implemented without first checking stationarity, then a spurious regress may be produced that could fail to reflect the actual trend in reality. Therefore, in order to circumvent this circumstance, Eviews 6.0 was used to perform a unit root test to assess stationarity. The results of the ADF tests are demonstrated hereunder for one country after another. See Figure 2.

(i) Augmented Dickey-Fuller Tests

Augmented Dickey-Fuller Unit Root Test on RUS_LEDU			Augmented Dickey-Fuller Unit Root Test on RUS_LGDP		
Null Hypothesis: RUS_LEDU has a unit root			Null Hypothesis: RUS_LGDP has a unit root		
Exogenous: Constant, Linear Trend			Exogenous: Constant, Linear Trend		
Lag Length: 2 (Automatic based on SIC, MAXLAG=4)			Lag Length: 0 (Automatic based on SIC, MAXLAG=4)		
	t-Statistic	Prob.*		t-Statistic	Prob.*
Augmented Dickey-Fuller test statistic	-3.195484	0.0372	Augmented Dickey-Fuller test statistic	-3.237647	0.0334
Test critical values: 1% level	-3.857386		Test critical values: 1% level	-3.808546	
5% level	-3.040391		5% level	-3.020686	
10% level	-2.660551		10% level	-2.650413	
*MacKinnon (1996) one-sided p-values.			*MacKinnon (1996) one-sided p-values.		

Figure 2– The outcome of the ADF test for the Russian LEDU, LGDP

Variable Name	ADF Statistics	P-value	Conclusion
RUS_LEDU	-3.195	0.037	Stationary
RUS_LGDP	-3.238	0.033	Stationary

Table 1– The results of the ADF test for the Russian data

The results have clearly shown that both time series for Russia have passed the ADF test since the p-values are both significantly less than the 0.05 critical level, thus rejecting the null hypothesis of having a unit root. The next step will be directly examining the possible causality between the Russian higher educational size and the country's economic expansion. See Figure 3.

Figure 3– The outcome of the ADF test for the BrazilianLEDU, LGDP & their 1st difference

Variable Name	ADF Statistics	P-value	Conclusion
BRA_LEDU	-1.316	0.601	Non-stationary
BRA_LGDP	-0.164	0.929	Non-stationary

△BRA_LEDU	-3.104	0.043	Stationary
△BRA_LGDP	-5.862	0.000	Stationary

Table 2 – The results of the ADF test for the Brazilian data

From the above results, we can see that the original two time series have not passed the ADF Test, therefore they are non-stationary. However, after taking the first difference, the p-values of the tests have become less than the 5% significance level, indicating that these series are integrated of order one. Thus we might expect a co-integration relationship between Brazilian's higher educational expansion and the country's economic development. See Figure 4.

Figure 4– The outcome of the ADF test for the IndianLEDU, LGDP & their 1st difference

Variable Name	ADF Statistics	P-value	Conclusion
IND_LEDU	-0.278	0.912	Non-stationary
IND_LGDP	0.923	0.994	Non-stationary

△IND_LEDU	-3.841	0.013	Stationary
△IND_LGDP	-3.076	0.046	Stationary

Table 3– The results of the ADF test for the Indian data

Likewise, the ADF test with constant term with a linear trend setting has demonstrated that the original series are not stationary. However, India's LEDU and LGDP are found to be integrated of order one as their first-differenced series are stationary. Thus, it is also possible that a co-integration relationship could exist between these two variables. See Figure 5.

Augmented Dickey-Fuller Unit Root Test on CHN_LEDU				Augmented Dickey-Fuller Unit Root Test on D(CHN_LEDU)			
Null Hypothesis: CHN_LEDU has a unit root				Null Hypothesis: D(CHN_LEDU) has a unit root			
Exogenous: Constant, Linear Trend				Exogenous: Constant, Linear Trend			
Lag Length: 2 (Automatic based on SIC, MAXLAG=4)				Lag Length: 1 (Automatic based on SIC, MAXLAG=4)			
		t-Statistic	Prob.*			t-Statistic	Prob.*
Augmented Dickey-Fuller test statistic		-0.484612	0.8731	Augmented Dickey-Fuller test statistic		-3.708676	0.0135
Test critical values:	1% level	-3.857386		Test critical values:	1% level	-3.857386	
	5% level	-3.040391			5% level	-3.040391	
	10% level	-2.660551			10% level	-2.660551	
*MacKinnon (1996) one-sided p-values.				*MacKinnon (1996) one-sided p-values.			
Augmented Dickey-Fuller Unit Root Test on CHN_LGDP				Augmented Dickey-Fuller Unit Root Test on D(CHN_LGDP)			
Null Hypothesis: CHN_LGDP has a unit root				Null Hypothesis: D(CHN_LGDP) has a unit root			
Exogenous: Constant, Linear Trend				Exogenous: Constant, Linear Trend			
Lag Length: 0 (Automatic based on SIC, MAXLAG=4)				Lag Length: 0 (Automatic based on SIC, MAXLAG=4)			
		t-Statistic	Prob.*			t-Statistic	Prob.*
Augmented Dickey-Fuller test statistic		-0.374281	0.8962	Augmented Dickey-Fuller test statistic		-3.242400	0.0331
Test critical values:	1% level	-3.808546		Test critical values:	1% level	-3.831511	
	5% level	-3.020686			5% level	-3.029970	
	10% level	-2.650413			10% level	-2.655194	
*MacKinnon (1996) one-sided p-values.				*MacKinnon (1996) one-sided p-values.			

Figure 5– The outcome of the ADF test for the Chinese LEDU, LGDP & their 1st difference

Variable Name	ADF Statistics	P-value	Conclusion
CHN_LEDU	-0.485	0.873	Non-stationary
CHN_LGDP	-0.374	0.896	Non-stationary
△CHN_LEDU	-3.709	0.014	Stationary
△CHN_LGDP	-3.242	0.033	Stationary

Table 4– The results of the ADF test for the Chinese data

The Chinese LEDU and LGDP series are found to be neither stationary, however their first differences both have stationary features. Thereupon, these two variables are also integrated of order one and it would be logical to continue to the next step for the co-integration test. See Figure 6.

Augmented Dickey-Fuller Unit Root Test on ZAF_LEDU			Augmented Dickey-Fuller Unit Root Test on ZAF_LGDP		
Null Hypothesis: ZAF_LEDU has a unit root Exogenous: Constant, Linear Trend Lag Length: 2 (Automatic based on SIC, MAXLAG=4)			Null Hypothesis: ZAF_LGDP has a unit root Exogenous: Constant, Linear Trend Lag Length: 0 (Automatic based on SIC, MAXLAG=4)		
	t-Statistic	Prob.*		t-Statistic	Prob.*
Augmented Dickey-Fuller test statistic	-3.235508	0.0345	Augmented Dickey-Fuller test statistic	-3.291155	0.0301
Test critical values: 1% level	-3.857386		Test critical values: 1% level	-3.808546	
5% level	-3.040391		5% level	-3.020686	
10% level	-2.660551		10% level	-2.650413	
*MacKinnon (1996) one-sided p-values.			*MacKinnon (1996) one-sided p-values.		

Figure 6– The outcome of the ADF test for the South African LEDU and LGDP

Variable Name	ADF Statistics	P-value	Conclusion
ZAF_LEDU	-3.236	0.035	Stationary
ZAF_LGDP	-3.291	0.030	Stationary

Table 5– The results of the ADF test for the South African data

The results have demonstrated a perfect statistical fit for stationarity, and therefore the examination of causality relationships between tertiary educational expansion and economic progress can be studied next under the South African context.

(ii) Co-integration Tests

As can be seen from the above section, the original time series of Brazil, India and China are not stationary per se. Nevertheless, the first differences of LEDU and

LGDP of these countries have all become stationary. I will use the Engle-Granger Two-step Test to examine if there is a co-integration relationship between the scale of tertiary education and economic advancement in each of these three BRICS countries. The Eviews 6.0 produced the following results. See Figure 7.

Dependent Variable: BRA_LGDP
Method: Least Squares
Date: 04/17/17   Time: 14:08
Sample: 1994 2014
Included observations: 21

Variable	Coefficient	Std. Error	t-Statistic	Prob.
BRA_LEDU	0.363943	0.019548	18.61817	0.0000
C	2.304920	0.050872	45.30821	0.0000

R-squared	0.948036	Mean dependent var	3.248571
Adjusted R-squared	0.945301	S.D. dependent var	0.085515
S.E. of regression	0.020000	Akaike info criterion	-4.895758
Sum squared resid	0.007600	Schwarz criterion	-4.796280
Log likelihood	53.40546	Hannan-Quinn criter.	-4.874169
F-statistic	346.6362	Durbin-Watson stat	0.332175
Prob(F-statistic)	0.000000		

Augmented Dickey-Fuller Unit Root Test on RESID01

Null Hypothesis: RESID01 has a unit root
Exogenous: Constant, Linear Trend
Lag Length: 0 (Automatic based on SIC, MAXLAG=4)

		t-Statistic	Prob.*
Augmented Dickey-Fuller test statistic		-1.171063	0.8891
Test critical values:	1% level	-4.498307	
	5% level	-3.658446	
	10% level	-3.268973	

*MacKinnon (1996) one-sided p-values.

Figure 7– The outcome of the Engle-Granger test for the Brazilian LEDU and LGDP

The linear regression result for the Brazilian case can be written as

$$BRA\_LGDP= 2.305 + 0.364\ BRA\_LEDU$$

$$(45.308) \qquad (18.618)$$

$$R^2 = 0.948 \qquad F\text{-Statistic}= 346.636$$

Both two estimated coefficients are highly significant as the P-values are below 5%. The Engle-Granger test examines the residual series and check if it is stationary. The t-Statistic for the ADF test for the residual series is -1.171, and the corresponding probability level is 0.889, which is far beyond the 5% significance level. Therefore, the Brazilian data have failed to demonstrate a co-integration relationship between the size of higher education and economic advancement. See Figure 8.

Dependent Variable: IND_LGDP
Method: Least Squares
Date: 04/17/17 Time: 14:22
Sample: 1994 2014
Included observations: 21

Variable	Coefficient	Std. Error	t-Statistic	Prob.
IND_LEDU	0.710992	0.022731	31.27916	0.0000
C	0.837034	0.070365	11.89556	0.0000
R-squared	0.980950	Mean dependent var		3.030952
Adjusted R-squared	0.979948	S.D. dependent var		0.182096
S.E. of regression	0.025786	Akaike info criterion		-4.387575
Sum squared resid	0.012633	Schwarz criterion		-4.288097
Log likelihood	48.06954	Hannan-Quinn criter.		-4.365986
F-statistic	978.3859	Durbin-Watson stat		0.770563
Prob(F-statistic)	0.000000			

Augmented Dickey-Fuller Unit Root Test on RESID03

Null Hypothesis: RESID03 has a unit root
Exogenous: Constant, Linear Trend
Lag Length: 4 (Automatic based on SIC, MAXLAG=4)

		t-Statistic	Prob.*
Augmented Dickey-Fuller test statistic		-5.221527	0.0039
Test critical values:	1% level	-4.667883	
	5% level	-3.733200	
	10% level	-3.310349	

*MacKinnon (1996) one-sided p-values.

Figure 8– The outcome of the Engle-Granger test for the Indian LEDU and LGDP

The linear regression result for the Indian case can be written as

$$IND\_LGDP = 0.837 + 0.711 \; IND\_LEDU$$

$$(11.896) \qquad (31.279)$$

$$R^2 = 0.980 \qquad F\text{-Statistic} = 978.386$$

The estimated linear regression is statistically meaningful as both coefficients are highly significant. The ADF test for the null hypothesis that the residual series of the regression line has a unit root is also highly significant, therefore indicating a co-integration relationship between the Indian educational expansion and the country's economic development. See Figure 9.

Dependent Variable: CHN_LGDP
Method: Least Squares
Date: 04/17/17 Time: 14:18
Sample: 1994 2014
Included observations: 21

Variable	Coefficient	Std. Error	t-Statistic	Prob.
CHN_LEDU	0.755257	0.037701	20.03255	0.0000
C	1.133125	0.119931	9.448141	0.0000
R-squared	0.954795	Mean dependent var		3.523333
Adjusted R-squared	0.952415	S.D. dependent var		0.254781
S.E. of regression	0.055578	Akaike info criterion		-2.851676
Sum squared resid	0.058689	Schwarz criterion		-2.752198
Log likelihood	31.94260	Hannan-Quinn criter.		-2.830087
F-statistic	401.3031	Durbin-Watson stat		0.227901
Prob(F-statistic)	0.000000			

Augmented Dickey-Fuller Unit Root Test on RESID02

Null Hypothesis: RESID02 has a unit root
Exogenous: Constant, Linear Trend
Lag Length: 1 (Automatic based on SIC, MAXLAG=4)

		t-Statistic	Prob.*
Augmented Dickey-Fuller test statistic		-4.566697	0.0183
Test critical values:	1% level	-4.532598	
	5% level	-3.673616	
	10% level	-3.277364	

*MacKinnon (1996) one-sided p-values.

Figure 9– The outcome of the Engle-Granger test for the Chinese LEDU and LGDP

The estimated relationship between the Chinese LEDU and LGDP can be found to be

$$CHN\_LGDP = 1.133 + 0.755 \, CHN\_LEDU$$

$$(9.448) \qquad (20.033)$$

$$R^2 = 0.955 \qquad \text{F-Statistic} = 401.303$$

The projected coefficients are both highly significant as reflected by the low P-value. The null hypothesis of a unit root in the residue series is also rejected because the ADF test produced a t-Statistic of -4.567, which is highly significant under the 5% level. Thus, it is reasonable to conclude that there is a co-integration relationship between the Chinese tertiary educational enrollment size and the country's rapid economic growth.

(iii) Granger Causality Tests

The previous sections have found that the Russian and South African time series are stationary without making any adjustment in lags. Thus, there is a stable long-term trend for both countries in terms of tertiary education and economic expansion. When it comes to India and China, the time series of higher education and the representative GDP are integrated of order one, and there is a co-integration relationship between LEDU and LGDP. Generally speaking, Granger Causality Test can be used to examine if one variable helps to predict and in a certain way cause the other variable to change in a period of time, and this fits well with the research question of this project. It is also believed that there is a hysteretic nature between the tertiary education development and the growth of the economy; therefore two lags have been selected according to convention and the BIC (Schwarz) Criterion has also been taken into account when using Eviews 6.0 to perform the Granger Causality Tests for the respective countries. In addition, the Brazilian time series are neither stationary nor co-integrated, suggesting an unstable relationship between the variables. Thus it would be meaningless to continue with the Granger Causality Test to figure out the possible causal relationship between these Brazilian variables in question. See Figure 10.

Pairwise Granger Causality Tests
Date: 04/17/17 Time: 13:27
Sample: 1994 2014
Lags: 2

Null Hypothesis:	Obs	F-Statistic	Prob.
RUS_LGDP does not Granger Cause RUS_LEDU	19	5.24224	0.0200
RUS_LEDU does not Granger Cause RUS_LGDP		3.34288	0.0650

Figure 10– The outcome of the Granger Causality test for the Russian LEDU and LGDP

From the Eviews 6.0 output, it is clear that from 1994 to 2014 the probability of Russia's economic development not being the Granger Causality of the Russian higher educational expansion is 2.00%, indicating that under the 5% significance level we should reject the null hypothesis. Conversely, during the same period of time, there is a 6.50% probability that the scale of Russian higher education does not Granger Cause Russia's economic advancement. At the conventional 5% significance level, we fail to reject the null hypothesis. See Figure 11.

21

Pairwise Granger Causality Tests
Date: 04/17/17 Time: 16:22
Sample: 1994 2014
Lags: 2

Null Hypothesis:	Obs	F-Statistic	Prob.
IND_LGDP does not Granger Cause IND_LEDU	19	5.11653	0.0215
IND_LEDU does not Granger Cause IND_LGDP		1.85496	0.1929

Figure11– The outcome of the Granger Causality test for the Indian LEDU and

LGDP

The Eviews 6.0 result clearly indicates that the probability of India's economic

expansion not Granger Causing the country's higher educational enrollment growth is

2.15%, which is far below the 5% significance level, thus we should confidently

reject the null hypothesis. However, when it comes to the probability that India's

higher education expansion does not Granger Cause the nation's economic growth, it

is multiple times higher, amounting to 19.29%, a percentage higher than the 5%

significance level. We fail to reject the second null hypothesis in the Indian case. See

Figure 12.

Pairwise Granger Causality Tests
Date: 04/17/17 Time: 16:13
Sample: 1994 2014
Lags: 2

Null Hypothesis:	Obs	F-Statistic	Prob.
CHN_LGDP does not Granger Cause CHN_LEDU	19	1.44010	0.2840
CHN_LEDU does not Granger Cause CHN_LGDP		10.2597	0.0016

Figure 12– The outcome of the Granger Causality test for the Chinese LEDU and

LGDP

Different than the previous two scenarios, the Granger Causality for the Chinese data is the other way round. The probability that China's economic expansion does not have Granger Cause the expansion of Chinese higher education is 28.40%, which is extremely insignificant even at the 10% significance level. However, there is a 0.16% probability that China's increased higher education enrollment does not Granger Cause the country's economic progress. In this case, it is appropriate to reject the null hypothesis and conclude that CHN_LEDU Granger Causes CHN_LGDP in the period from 1994 to 2014. See Figure 13.

Pairwise Granger Causality Tests
Date: 04/17/17 Time: 13:29
Sample: 1994 2014
Lags: 2

Null Hypothesis:	Obs	F-Statistic	Prob.
ZAF_LGDP does not Granger Cause ZAF_LEDU	19	0.71660	0.6038
ZAF_LEDU does not Granger Cause ZAF_LGDP		4.14114	0.0416

Figure 13– The outcome of the Granger Causality test for the South African LEDU and LGDP

The Eviews 6.0 result has demonstrated a statistically meaningful Granger Causality in which South African tertiary education expansion Granger Causes the improvement in South Africa's economic advancement since the P-value for this hypothesis testing stands at 4.16%, which is below the 5% significance level and it is

23

safe to reject the null hypothesis. The probability that South African economic growth does not Granger Cause the country's improved higher education enrollment is more than 60%, which is extremely insignificant, leading to the failure of rejecting the null hypothesis.

b. Research Question 2

The second research question deals with the impact of the layer structure of higher education to the economic development. The dependent variable log of GDP represents economic progress. Two independent variables including the log of EDU and the log of VOE have been used to differentiate the impact level each layer of higher education brings to the economy. The magnitude and the significance level of each variable will be the primary focus in this section. Stata 13.0 was used to run the simple linear regression for each respective BRICS country taking into account of a time frame of 21 years commencing 1994 and ending 2014. The result is demonstrated in Figure 14 as follows.

(i) Russia

```
. import excel "C:\Users\windows8\Desktop\Êý¾Ý\Regression\RUS_1994-2014.xls", sh
> eet("Sheet3") firstrow clear

. regress LGDP LEDU LVOE, robust

Linear regression                                   Number of obs =      21
                                                    F(  2,     18) =   80.33
                                                    Prob > F       =  0.0000
                                                    R-squared      =  0.8532
                                                    Root MSE       =   .0466
```

LGDP	Coef.	Robust Std. Err.	t	P>|t|	[95% Conf. Interval]	
LEDU	1.144486	.1196526	9.57	0.000	.8931048	1.395866
LVOE	-1.211789	.2693702	-4.50	0.000	-1.777715	-.645863
_cons	2.502764	.3434847	7.29	0.000	1.78113	3.224399

Figure 14– The linear regression output in Stata13.0 for the Russian data

The output indicates that the relationship among Russian economic expansion, academic higher education program size and tertiary vocational training enrollment is as follows.

$$RUS\_LGDP = 2.503 + 1.144\ RUS\_LEDU - 1.212\ RUS\_LVOE$$

$$(7.29) \qquad\qquad (9.57) \qquad\qquad\qquad (-4.50)$$

$$R^2 = 0.85 \qquad\qquad F\text{-Statistic} = 80.33$$

All coefficients are estimated to be highly significant even at the 1% significance level provided that they associated P-values are almost close to 0%. It is worth noting that the coefficient of RUS_LVOE is found to be negative while being significant. In comparison, RUS_LEDU exerts a positive impact to Russia's economic advancement within the time frame studied. The R squared parameter is within the reasonable range, therefore the regression line is a close fit to the original time series. See Figure 15.

(ii) Brazil

```
. import excel "C:\Users\windows8\Desktop\Êý¾Ý\Regression\BRA_1994-2014.xls", sh
> eet("Sheet2") firstrow clear

. regress LGDP LEDU LVOE, robust

Linear regression                               Number of obs =       21
                                                F( 2,    18) =   465.67
                                                Prob > F      =   0.0000
                                                R-squared     =   0.9842
                                                Root MSE      =   .01134
```

LGDP	Coef.	Robust Std. Err.	t	P>|t|	[95% Conf. Interval]	
LEDU	.4198209	.0144575	29.04	0.000	.3894468	.450195
LVOE	.0773872	.0111035	6.97	0.000	.0540596	.1007149
_cons	1.996786	.0529109	37.74	0.000	1.885624	2.107947

Figure 15 – The linear regression output in Stata13.0 for the Brazilian data

The linear regression model can be thus written as follows

BRA_LGDP = 1.997 + 0.420 BRA_LEDU + 0.077 BRA_LVOE

(37.74)   (29.04)   (6.97)

$R^2 = 0.98$ F-Statistic= 465.67

The estimated coefficients are all significant even at the 1% significance level, since the P-values are all quite close to 0% and less than 1%. The coefficients of the academic higher education size and also the vocational higher education size are both positive, indicating a positive impact that these two variables bring to the country's economy. The R squared parameter also suggests that the regression result is a good fit to the original time series. See Figure 16.

(iii) India

26

```
. import excel "C:\Users\windows8\Desktop\Êý*Ý\Regression\IND_1994-2014.xls", sh
> eet("Sheet2") firstrow clear

. regress LGDP LEDU LVOE, robust
```

Linear regression

Number of obs = 21
F(2, 18) = 813.88
Prob > F = 0.0000
R-squared = 0.9837
Root MSE = .02448

LGDP	Coef.	Robust Std. Err.	t	P>|t|	[95% Conf. Interval]	
LEDU	.6695966	.0253819	26.38	0.000	.6162712	.7229219
LVOE	.1034701	.0498856	2.07	0.053	-.0013355	.2082758
_cons	.7661553	.0669186	11.45	0.000	.6255646	.906746

Figure 16 – The linear regression output in Stata13.0 for the Indian data

The linear regression model derived from the Stata13.0 output can be written as follows.

$$\text{IND\_LGDP} = 0.766 + 0.670 \text{ IND\_LEDU} + 0.103 \text{ IND\_LVOE}$$

$$(11.45) \qquad (26.38) \qquad (2.07)$$

$$R^2 = 0.98 \qquad \text{F-Statistic} = 813.88$$

The estimated coefficients of IND_LEDU and the constant term are both highly significant with P-values being less than even the 1% significance level. However, the coefficient of IND_LVOE is barely significant; the associated P-value is slightly higher than the conventional 5% significance level. The enrollment of academic program at higher education and also the vocational program both contribute positively to India's economic expansion. The R squared level is 0.98, indicating a good fit with the original Indian data over the time span studied.

(iv) China

```
. import excel "C:\Users\windows8\Desktop\Êý¾Ý\Regression\CHN_1994-2014.xls", sh
> eet("Sheet2") firstrow clear

. regress LGDP LEDU LVOE, robust

Linear regression                              Number of obs =        21
                                               F(  2,    18) =    390.79
                                               Prob > F      =    0.0000
                                               R-squared     =    0.9805
                                               Root MSE      =    .03753

                           Robust
       LGDP |     Coef.   Std. Err.      t    P>|t|     [95% Conf. Interval]
------------+----------------------------------------------------------------
       LEDU |   .474458    .0499038    9.51   0.000     .3696141    .579302
       LVOE |  .7849378    .1219961    6.43   0.000     .5286334   1.041242
      _cons | -.4507673    .2648273   -1.70   0.106    -1.007149   .1056141
```

Figure 17– The linear regression output in Stata13.0 for the Chinese data

The linear model for the Chinese data can be written as follows.

CHN_LGDP = $-0.451 + 0.474$ CHN_LEDU $+ 0.785$ CHN_LVOE

$\qquad\qquad$ (-1.70) $\qquad\qquad$ (9.51) $\qquad\qquad\qquad$ (6.43)

$R^2 = 0.98$ $\qquad\qquad$ F-Statistic= 390.71

The estimated coefficients of CHN_LEDU and CHN_LVOE are both highly
significant as their associated P-values are even smaller than the 1% significance
level. Since their coefficients are both positive, therefore China's increased
enrollment in the tertiary education in both academic and vocational programs have a
positive impact on the growth of the nation's economy. This model was also well
estimated and a good fit to the original data since the R squared parameter is quite
high, amounting to 0.98. See Figure 18.

(v) South Africa

```
.  import excel "C:\Users\windows8\Desktop\ĚŷŁŸ\Regression\ZAF_1994-2014.xls", sh
>  eet("Sheet2") firstrow clear

.  regress LGDP LEDU LVOE, robust

Linear regression                                 Number of obs =        21
                                                  F(  2,   18) =    699.64
                                                  Prob > F      =    0.0000
                                                  R-squared     =    0.9831
                                                  Root MSE      =    .01183
```

LGDP	Coef.	Robust Std. Err.	t	P>|t|	[95% Conf. Interval]	
LEDU	1.34852	.0574442	23.48	0.000	1.227834	1.469205
LVOE	-.0514936	.0165775	-3.11	0.006	-.0863216	-.0166656
_cons	-.0247207	.0935747	-0.26	0.795	-.2213139	.1718725

Figure 18– The linear regression output in Stata13.0 for the South African data

In the case of South Africa, the simple linear relationship among economic development, enrollment in academic program of higher education and the participation level in vocational training at the tertiary level looks as follows.

$$ZAF\_LGDP = -0.025 + 1.349\ ZAF\_LEDU\ -0.051\ ZAF\_LVOE$$

$$(-0.26) \qquad\qquad (23.48) \qquad\qquad\qquad (-3.11)$$

$$R^2 = 0.98 \qquad\qquad \text{F-Statistic} = 699.64$$

The coefficients of ZAF_LEDU and ZAF_LVOE prove to be useful for statistical inferences since their associated P-values are both even less than the 1% significance level. From the period studied, the estimated coefficient of LEDU is positive while the counterpart of LVOE is slightly negative; suggesting a rather different effect the

29

increase in enrollment into these two tertiary programs brings to the South African economy. This regression model can also be considered as a good fit to the original data since the R squared parameter is 0.98.

6. Evaluation and Discussions

a. Russia

The Augmented Dickey-Fuller (ADF) Test has demonstrated that both the log term of the Russian tertiary enrollment and also the Russian economic expansion are both stationary time series and there is no seasonality involved. There is a time lag effect in the interaction between these two variables, namely the changes of one variable would impact the other variable after a period of time rather than simultaneously. The BIC (Schwarz) Criterion selected a lag of 3. Statistically speaking, the Granger Causality test has shown that the country's economic development was the Granger Causality for the increased higher education enrollment during the time period studied. Conversely, higher education expansion did not significantly Granger Cause the Russian economic growth as the P-value narrowly marginally missed the 5% threshold. Therefore, the statistical output indicates a unidirectional Causality relationship and thus it is incompatible with the hypothesis since no simultaneous Granger Causality between the Russian tertiary enrollment size and the Russian economic expansion was found. However, it is not correct to deny the role higher education plays in the course of economic growth. Among all BRICS nations, the

Russian Federation had a relatively solid foundation in the provision of education. In the period around 1990s, the Soviet Union had already invested more than 2.5% of the GDP to develop education, and the 11-year course program which includes a free university level education had officially been executed throughout the union nation in 1991 and was carried forward later in other Commonwealth of Independent States (In Russian: СодружествоНезависимыхГосударств) (OEDC, 2016). The Russian government also invested heavily and allocated sufficient funding for universities since the commencement of the 1990s, the state-owned tertiary institutions were rising steadily from around 514 at the beginning to 655 in the new millennium; similarly, the number of private tertiary institutions also rose from 193 to more than 280 in 2006 (Ministry of Education and Science of the Russian Federation, 2008). Another effect of the increased government subsidy to the increase in higher education enrollment is that the Russian gross tertiary enrollment ratio has been consistently more than 70% in the past decade – being consistently at the top among other BRICS counterparts and even also significantly higher than the OCED average enrollment rate while also maintaining a relatively smaller class size (OECD, 2012). As regards the second research question, we can take a look at the regression model outcome concerning two different realms and make comparisons based on several indicators. First of all, both the academic program and the vocational training program at the tertiary level make significant impact to the country's economic growth within the time period studied, while also noting that the academic training was estimated to be able to make a larger impact. When the size of the academic program stays the same, then increase in enrollment to vocational tertiary institutions would significantly decrease Russia's economic growth. In recent years, the information technology is one of the most dynamic highlights in the country. The most important subsectors focus on network integration and the ever growing offshore programming. Among BRICS, Russia is also an active offshore software development market after China and India and the market is still growing at a remarkable rate of 35% (The Economist, 2012). In addition, a non-negligible portion of the enrolled tertiary vocational students are previously conscripted and have to perform military service before applying to university academic programs, which sometimes make them disadvantaged in the academic competition due to less time spent on academic exploration. Therefore, these reasons contribute to the regression result that academic tertiary programs contribute more positively than the vocational tertiary programs do to Russia's economic expansion.

b. Brazil

It was found that both the original time series of the Brazilian log of GDP and also the log of higher education enrollment are not stationary in the first place. The result of the first differenced ADF Test has shown that they become stationary, meaning that they have time term trends and are stable. However, the Engle-Granger Test has demonstrated that the residual series of the linear regression model has a large P-value which is highly insignificant, resulting in the non-existence of a co-integration relationship. If there is no co-integration relationship, then it would be meaningless to analyze the statistical causality between the variables in question since the Granger Causality test has a prerequisite that the time series should be either stationary or be integrated of the same order. Therefore, it would not be possible to tell whether the hypothesis of a simultaneous Granger Causality should be rejected or not. However, the Engle-Granger equation has shown that the coefficient of the Brazilian higher education enrollment stays positive and contributes to the economic expansion of the country. Nonetheless, since there is no long-term equilibrium, precisely which factor Granger Causes another is difficult to seek. After suffering from stagnation, inflation and various crises from 1981 to 1993, Brazil adopted a "Real Plan" in the spring of 1994 in an attempt to break inflationary expectation and improve the current account deficits. The economy of Brazil set to be on the right track with the maintenance of tight fiscal and monetary policy. During the same time period, the number of the tertiary education institutions was also on the rise, in particular the private colleges and those in the field of engineering and technology. During the decade before the new millennium, Brazil drafted several policies to improve national education, for example the 1991's "Education Revolution" campaign. Nevertheless most of the efforts were in vain as the government still falls short of investment and funding in developing education. The average allocated funds to general education accounted for less than 5% of the total GDP, which is significantly lower than other South American states and also the OECD average rate (Wang, 2007). Thus the increasing provision of higher education cannot be credited to the government but would be from other sources of finance from other lucrative sectors in the economy where they are more of a private-owned nature. It could then be argued that economic advancement and tertiary enrollment interacted positively with each other in Brazil as more private institutions were made available thank to the economic expansion, and the talents cultivated by the higher education institutions later contribute back to the industrial upgrading of the country. The second research question looks into the effect of the break-down of the Brazilian higher education sector. The linear regression result has demonstrated that both the tertiary academic programs and the tertiary vocational training programs contribute positively to the country's economic expansion. However, the academic programs exerted a much larger positive effect than the vocational training programs do. Brazil has abundant natural resources with one of the largest supply of nickel, bauxite, copper and gold within the region. Brazilian tertiary vocational programs are coordinated nationwide through the National Industrial Training Centre in Brasilia, the aim of which is to train qualified workers in the field of electronics, auto-control and mining (Wang, 2005). These workers will later contribute significantly to the resource oriented sectors and economic growth. However, the largest percentage of labor force is in the country's service sector, accounting for more than 70% in 2011. Moreover, Brazil has been undergoing a significant wave of industrial upgrading that pays special attention to the new energy sector that is based upon the abundance of natural resources in the country. Academic training at the tertiary level is crucial to the provision of talents who would later work in areas such as green finance, ecological preservation as well as renewable energy. Academic tertiary programs can be deemed investments in scientific research that prove to be a valuable deal since innovation is the key to a country's long-term sustainable growth. Thereupon, it is not difficult to understand that academic training provided Brazil a much powerful momentum in terms of the country's economic expansion.

c. India

The Indian log of higher education time series and the log of GDP are not stationary in the time frame studied, thus the original time series are not stable. However, after taking the first difference, both time series become statistically stationary, thereupon a long-term co-integration relationship might exist between these two variables. The co-integration function has shown that the higher educational size contributed positively to the economic development in the context of India. The non-unit root feature of the residual time series indicates co-integration and it has demonstrated a long-term equilibrium between Indian higher education enrollment and Indian economic expansion. The Granger Causality test then found out that in the time period between 1994 and 2014 the country's economic expansion Granger Caused the increasing higher education enrollment. However, the Granger Causality from the rising tertiary enrollment to the economic expansion does not exist from a statistical point of view. Consequently, this rejects the earlier hypothesis that there would be a bidirectional statistical Causality between the two variables. Ever since India gained independence from the British rule in 1947, the country invested heavily in the cultivation of science and engineering talents, who were often the major contributors in the post-independence construction periods. India then carried forward such tradition and kept focusing on the higher education sector. Although from 1947 to 1991, the growth rate of the Indian economy was quite unfavorable. This period was often characterized as the "Hindu rate growth period" as the nation simultaneously concentrated on capital intensive and heavy technology industries and also subsidized various low-skill manual work industries. The post-liberalization period commencing 1991 has led to a favorable turn in India's economic development. The government terminated a number of public monopolies and reformed labor law and transformed India into a more market based free economy. India then entered a period of high growth, with the growth rate averaging around 6% later up to 2007. During the *Indian Eighth Plan* (1992-1997) period, industrial modernization was the cornerstone of the government blueprint. To further strengthen the infrastructure construction and to increase employability for the fellow citizens, Indian government decided to increase the allocation of funds to the education sector by 6.2%, with special emphasis on science and technology curriculum at the tertiary level (Agrawal, 2005, p.676). These concrete investments led to the expansion of higher education institutions which include 152 central universities and 316 state universities by 2012 (Singh and Nath, 2013, p.173). Thus the Granger Causality direction is corroborated. The second research question looks into the differentiating effects brought about by the two spheres of higher education. The regression output has demonstrated that both academic tertiary education and also vocational programs at the tertiary level contributed positively over the period of interest. It is also worth noting that increased academic tertiary enrollment had a much larger effect than the vocational training did. India is the second largest economy in BRICS with one of the fastest growth in the service sector with an annual growth rate of slightly more than 9% ever since the new millennium. The country is renowned for the excellence in software engineering, petrochemicals and pharmaceuticals. Academic research-oriented universities such as Indian Institute of Technology and Indian Institute of Science are globally recognized and they produce outstanding graduates in engineering and chemistry. These graduates work in the field of basic research that further boosts innovation in the country and make India be able to grow its economy smoothly more sustainably. India's vocational tertiary education in infrastructure, town services and engineering plays a minor role in the economic advancement. Anand (2011)'s study pointed out that more than 75% vocational training graduates are short of the skills demanded in the country's high growth industries, leading to the suspicion of the quality of India's vocational training programs. It therefore makes more sense that increased enrollment in academic tertiary programs yields more than the vocational enrollment at the tertiary level for the benefit of India's national economic growth.

d. China

The log of China's higher education enrollment and the log of China's GDP are non-stationary, meaning that the original time series are not stable. However, the first differences of these two variables later become stationary, thus suggesting a possibility of a co-integration relationship. The Engle-Granger co-integration function has shown that during the period from 1994 to 2014 China's tertiary enrollment was positively correlated to the country's economic growth. The residual time series was also stationary. The co-integration theory asserts that there is a long-term stable equilibrium between Chinese tertiary enrollment and Chinese economic expansion along with a statistical causality between them. The stability here indicates that even if one of the two variables fluctuates, the ratio of these variables will be unaffected and remains to be stable. As can be seen from the Granger Causality Test, it is statistically significant to conclude that the increased Chinese tertiary enrollment Granger Caused the country's increasing economic output. It was a unidirectional Granger Causality since we failed to reject the null hypothesis that the Chinese gross economic output statistically caused the increased educational enrollment. Therefore the earlier hypothesis is rejected and the ideal scenario of a simultaneous Causality was not found. The major reason lies in the socioeconomic status in China back in history. The material basis is the primary foundation of societal development since it can provide sufficient resources and impetus for growth. At the outset of China's resumption of the National Higher Education Entrance Examination in 1977 which symbolized the restart of higher education enrollment, Chinese gross enrollment ratio to the tertiary level was only around 1%. China was in still in extreme poverty even before the period studied in the project with the national GDP per capita being only 348 US dollar in 1990. Owing not only to the shortage of funds, but also due to the long-standing institutional tradition, tertiary institutions in China have long been run and taken care of by the central government. Lacking a certain degree of autonomy, Chinese tertiary education institutions were often inactive in raising funds for self-development; but instead, they had a "planned economy" mindset that heavily depended on central government's funding. Though China's GDP started to increase with an unprecedented pace after 1991 and especially after 1992 when Deng Xiaoping decided to transform the country into a socialist market economy. However these hardly directed benefited the higher education sector. The main educational objective for the central government was to implement the "Nine-year Compulsory Education" program nationwide, thus primary and secondary education were actually the focal point of China at that time; since a significantly larger proportion of funding went to those areas (Zhu & Lou, 2011, p.47). Generally speaking, the enrollment to tertiary education can only be expanded when there are sufficient amount of students well educated at the secondary level. Therefore there is barely any statistically significant Granger Causality from China's GDP growth directly to the nation's size of enrollment in tertiary institutions. On the other hand, Chinese tertiary enrollment significantly Granger Caused the country's GDP expansion. With respect to the structure of tertiary education, both academic programs and the vocational training programs have a statistically significant effect on the GDP growth, of which the vocational training program played a larger part. China has abundant natural resources, thus producing vibrant iron, steel, aluminum and coal industries. Moreover, China is also widely recognized as the biggest hub for manufacturing. The country assembles the largest number of consumer products, which include toys, shoes, electronics, etc. By the turn of the new century, industrialization was taking place in the country in an unprecedented scale. Qualified technical workers were highly demanded by various industrial sectors in the economy. The increased enrollment in vocational training at the tertiary level would form a firm support of human capital. Therefore, it is not difficult to understand the regression result that increased tertiary vocational training had a relatively higher contribution ratio than the general tertiary academic program did to the Chinese economic expansion.

e. South Africa

Both the log of South African tertiary education enrollment and the log of GDP of South Africa between 1994 and 2014 are stationary time series. Therefore these variables are stable over time and do not have large fluctuations. The plots of South African LEDU and LGDP have shown that they were gradually growing at a smooth pace during the time frame. The Granger Causality test yields the unidirectional result. South Africa's enrollment in tertiary education Granger Caused the changes in South African economic expansion. However, the country's economic expansion did not statistically Granger Caused the changes in higher education enrollment. Therefore, it is evident that the hypothesis of a bidirectional Granger Causality is rejected and there was hardly any statistically significant dynamic interaction between the higher education sector and the country's economic output. 1994 can be regarded as a dividing line since South Africa brought to an end of the old republic and officially abandoned apartheid after Nelson Mandela assumed office. South Africa entered a period towards social democracy and economic modernization. The government revoked discriminatory policies and allowed non-white students to enroll in university study programs. In the period before, African children that account for the largest share of the youth population were not permitted to study with white children in public schools, resulting in a large number of illiterate populations and most of them ended up doing grueling mechanical low-end jobs. The situation turned better after 1994 and the government increased funding to around 20% of the annual fiscal budget in educational related causes, and a large portion of which went to primary and secondary level education that could well prepare students for studying at the tertiary education level. On the background of the industrialization transition, the *1997 South African Higher Education Act* set a concrete plan to increase the proportion of science and engineering students from 25% to 30% in the entire tertiary enrollment (Luo, 2007). Science graduates were often found in the fields of machinery, textile, steel and mining; and they are the major sectors underpinning the South African economy. During the period from 1994 to 2012, the South African GDP grew at an average growth rate of 3.25% and the GDP in 2012 was around 2.5% the GDP of 1974, indicating an economic success in the country's two decades of democracy. Thus it is reasonable to understand that the increased tertiary enrollment Granger Caused a wave of economic expansion in South Africa. It can be seen from the linear regression output that the academic tertiary program made positive contribution to South African economic growth while the effect of tertiary vocational training was marginally negative to the expansion of South African economy. The South African labor supply was ample, but there has been a significant structural unemployment in the country. More than 40% of tertiary vocational training graduates were unemployed in the 2011 census. Due to the enduring apartheid, most Africans could not afford a chance to receive proper secondary and tertiary education, resulting in more than 70% of the labor force being graduates from secondary or tertiary vocational training institutes (Spreen and Vally, 2006). The large pool of uneducated and unqualified graduates has dampened the willingness of foreign high tech firms to move into South Africa. In addition, after the financial crisis there was a shrinking demand for the low-end mechanical positions due to the withering mineral and mining industry. Moreover, the cost of manual labor in South Africa was also considered to be one of the highest among the BRICS countries. While it is found that manufacturing workers are more productive than their counterparts in other BRICS economies. Therefore, the structural unemployment for many graduates from tertiary vocational institutions could also be attributed to the higher labor cost, which is a financial burden for many local factories to hire more (Ardington, Case and Hosegood, 2007). The quality of the academic tertiary education in South Africa has been rising fast and there have been more international collaboration in research in the field of business management, science and technology, which is believed to be able to contribute to the sustainable development of the South African economy. Therefore, the directional impact and the scale of effects of the tertiary academic education and the tertiary vocational program to the country's economic expansion have been explained.

7. Conclusions

This project investigated the dynamics between tertiary education and the increasing economic output in the BRICS countries. Various statistical results have demonstrated that during the studied period, Russian and Indian economic expansion Granger Caused the increased tertiary enrollment in these two countries. While China and South Africa's higher education enrollment Granger Caused improvement in both countries' economic expansion. The Russian government has been consistently attaching importance to the higher education sector and the country had a long-standing tradition of funding the tertiary education since the Soviet time. Indian economy took off gradually after 1991; the favorable economic performance was deemed a catalyst for the increased enrollment in tertiary education. Having started from a very fragile foundation, China and South Africa's main tasks were to increase the provision of basic level education to the broad masses of the people before they were able to pay extra attention to the development of tertiary education. However, the university graduates especially those in the field of science and technology in China and South Africa made considerable contribution to the advancement of the economy by increasing productivity and supporting industrialization. Unfortunately, Brazil's Granger Causality could not be statistically figured out since the Brazilian data sets were neither stationary nor co-integrated of the same order. The actual results have been far from the ideal scenario, in which an interactive Granger Causality relationship was expected for each of the BRICS country. This project later sought to measure the effect of tertiary academic education and tertiary vocational education to the country's economic development. It is found that tertiary academic programs in every BRICS country contributed positively to the economic expansion within the time frame, while the impact of vocational training at the tertiary level exerted different effects. In Russia and South Africa, tertiary vocational education tended to lead to a negative shock to the national economy, in particular the negative impact level was significantly higher in Russia. Tertiary academic education in all BRICS countries except China is found to have a larger contribution ratio than the counterpart vocational training programs. Academic training at the higher education level could lead to more scientific discoveries and technology upgrading for the country, which serve as the foundation for sustainable development and contribute to economic expansion. The negative impact of tertiary vocational enrollment to the country's GDP was not originally anticipated, thus follow up research is suggested to include more observations that stretch across a wider time span. In addition, there are several drawbacks as regards the research setup and methodology in this project: Firstly: the yearly variation in each independent variable was not significant over a period of time, and the error term in the regression model might be correlated with the value in another year. This could violate the general assumptions of the regression model. In addition, the time lag effect is not fully taken into account to help make comparisons. Thirdly, the sample size upon which the results and analysis are based is too small. This study only takes into account of the time span of 21 years because the tertiary enrollment population before 1994 regardless of the academic or vocational nature can hardly be obtained for South Africa and India. Moreover, this project did not include other credible control variables in the course of estimating the dissimilar level of impact of tertiary educational structure to GDP expansion, thus possibly twisting the exact magnitude of impact. Thus future research could consider expanding the time frame by including more than 45 years of trustworthy data related to tertiary enrollment of different categories; in addition, other statistically significant results might also emerge should the time period be further divided into sub periods with each representing a specific strategic timing for each country over their course of higher education expansion and also their economic growth.

8. References

Agrawal, A. N. (2005) *Indian Economy: Problems of Development and Planning*. 31sted. New Delhi: New Age International Limited Publishers.

Anand, G. (2011) 'India Graduates Millions, but Too Few Are Fit to Hire', *The Wall Street Journal*, April, pp.12-18.

Ardichvili, A., Zavyalova, E. &Minina, V. (2012) 'Human Capital Development: Comparative Analysis of BRICs', *European Journal of Training and Development*, 36(2/3), pp.213-233.

Ardington, C., Case, A. &Hosegood, V. (2009) 'Labor Supply Responses to Large Social Transfers: Longitudinal Evidence from South Africa', *American Economic Journal: Applied Economics*, 1 (1), pp.22-48.

Autor, D. H., Katz, L. F. & Krueger, A.B. (1998) 'Computing inequality: Have computers changed the labor market?',*The Quarterly Journal of Economics*, 113(4),pp.1169–1213.

Badsha, N.& Nico, C. (2011)*Higher Education: Contribution for the NPC's National Development Plan*, Cape Town: Centre for Higher Education Transformation.

Barro, R. J. (1990) 'Government Spending in a Simple Model of Endogenous Growth', *Journal of Political Economy*, 98(1), pp.103-125.

Becker, G. (1978) *The Economic Approach to Human Behavior*, Chicago: University of Chicago Press.

Beddie, F.M. (2009)'Australia and India: Facing the Twenty-First Century Skills Challenge',*Annual Global Skills Summit: Emerging Skills — India 2020*, 20-21 August, New Delhi. Adelaide: National Centre for Vocational Education Research, pp.1-13.

Boughey, C. &McKenna, S. (2011) *A Meta-analysis of Teaching and Learning at Five Historically Disadvantaged Universities*, Pretoria: Council on Higher Education.

Card, D. (1999) 'The Causal Effect of Education on Earnings". In: Ashenfelter, O. C.& Card, D. (ed.) *Handbook of Labor Economics*,Amsterdam: Elsevier, pp.1801-1863.

Carnoy, M., Loyalka, P. &Froumin, I. (2013) 'University Expansion in the BRIC Countries and the Global Information Economy', *Change*, 45(4), July/August, pp.36-43.

Denison, E. F. (1985) *Trends in American Economic Growth, 1929-1982*. Washington DC: Brookings Institution.

Fan, M. (2006) *Higher Education and Coordinated Economic Development*. Beijing: Social Sciences Academic Press.

Foroohar, R. (2009) 'BRICs Overtake G7 By 2027',*China Market*, 20, p.70.

Freeman, R. B. (1976) *The Overeducated American*. New York: Academic Press.

Gao, D. (1998) 'Four Asian Tigers' Higher Educational Structure Adjustment for Economic Development', *Journal of Jinan University (Philosophy & Social Science Edition)*, 2, pp.119-124.

Goetz, S. J. &Rupasingha, A. (2003) 'The Returns on Higher Education: Estimates for the 48Contiguous States', *Economic Development Quarterly*, 17(4), pp.337-351.

Hao, K. & Wang, Y. (1987) *Research on Chinese Higher Educational Structure*. Beijing: People's Education Press.

Hult, T. (2009) 'The BRICs Countries', *Global Edge Business Review*, 3(4), pp.1-2.

Kosack, S. (2009) 'RealisingEducation for All: defining and using the political will to invest inprimary education', *Comparative Education*, 45(4), pp.495-523.

Kuznets, S. (1971) *Economic Growth of Nations:TotalOutputandProductionStructure*. Cambridge (USA): Harvard University Press.

Lewis, W. A. (1955) *The Theory of Economic Growth*. London: Allen and Unwin.

Lopes, G. P. (2015) 'The Sino-Brazilian principles in a Latin American and BRICS context: the case for comparative public budgeting legal research', *Wisconsin International Law Journal*, 33(1), p.1.

Lucas, R. E. (1988) 'On the Mechanics of Economic Development', *Journal of Monetary Economics*, 22(1), pp.3-42.

Luo, Y. (2007) 'South African Education Reform and Development', *West Asia and Africa*, 9, September, pp.17-22.

Lynham, S. A.& Cunningham, P. W. (2006)'National Human Resource Development in Transitioning Societies in the Developing World: Concept and Challenges', *Advances in Developing HumanResources*,8(1), pp.116-135.

Maddison, A. (1992) 'A Long-run Perspective on Saving', *Scandinavian Journal of Economics*, 94(2), pp.181-196.

Ma, D.& Mao, H. (2004) 'The Econometrics Analysis of the Relationship between Higher Education Development and Economic Growth', *Finance and Economics*, 202(1), pp.92-95.

McConnell, C.R.& Brue, S.L. (1988) *Contemporary Labour Economics*. 2nd ed. NewYork: McGraw-Hill.

Menon, E. M. (1997) 'Higher Education and the Post-modern Challenge', *Reflections on Higher Education*,9, pp.103-113.

Ministry of Education and Science of the Russian Federation. (2008) *Statistics: Tertiary Professional Education* [Online] Available from: http://www.ed.gov.ru/uprav/stat/1846/ (Accessed: 20 April 2017)

Nafukho, F.M., Hairston, N.R. & Brooks, K. (2004)'Human Capital Theory: Implications for Human Resource Development', *Human Resource Development International*,7(4),pp.545-551.

OECD. (2012) 'How Does Class Size Vary Around the World?',*Education Indicators in Focus*, 9, November, pp.1-4.

OECD. (2016) *Education at a Glance 2016: OECD Indicators – Russian Federation.* [Online] Paris: OECD Publishing. Available from:http://dx.doi.org/10.1787/eag-2016-en (Accessed: 20 April 2017)

O'Neill, J. (2001) *Building Better Global Economic BRICs*, Global Economics Paper no.66, New York,Goldman Sachs.

Romer, P. M. (1986) 'Increasing Returns and Long-run Growth', *Journal of Political Economy*, 94(5), pp.1002-1037.

Samuelson, P. A. (1948) *Economics, an Introductory Analysis*. New York: McGraw-Hill.

Schultz, T. W. (1960) 'Capital Formation by Education', *Journal of Political Economy*, 68(6), pp.571-583.

Schultz, T.W. (1961a) 'Education and economic growth'. In: Henry, N.B. (ed.)*Social   Forces Influencing American Education*. Chicago: University of Chicago Press, pp.46-88.

Schultz, T. W. (1961b) 'Investment in Human Capital',*The American EconomicReview*,51(1), pp.1–17.

Schwab, K. (2016) *The Global Competitiveness Report 2016-2017*, Geneva: The World Economic Forum.

Singh, Y. K. &Nath, R. (2013) *History of Indian Education System*. New Delhi: APH Publishing Corporation.

Smialek, J. (2015) *These Will Be the World's 20 Largest Economies in 2030* [Online]. Available from:

http://www.bloomberg.com/news/articles/2015-04-10/the-world-s-20-largest-economies-in-2030 (Accessed: 15 November 2016).

Spreen, C. A. &Vally, S. (2006) 'Education Rights, Education Policies and Inequality in South Africa', *International Journal of Educational Development*, 26 (4), pp.352-362.

The Economist. (2012) *The Internet Business in Russia: Europe's Great Exception*[Online] Moscow: The Economist Group. Available from: http://www.economist.com/node/21555560 (Accessed: 21 April 2017)

Wang, R. (2005) 'Education and Economic Development — A Comparative Study Between the United States and Brazil', *Journal of Inner Mongolia Normal University (Educational Science)*, 18 (5), May, pp.5-8.

Wang, Y. (2007) 'The Brazilian Education SectorMakes Impact to theNational Economic Development', *World Culture*, 9, September, p.34.

Ying, W. (2008) *Thirty Years of Chinese Higher Educational Reform and Development*. Shanghai: Shanghai University of Finance and Economics Press.

Zaharia, M., Popescu, C. &Feniser, C. (2016) 'The Structure of Active Population by Educational Levels before and after the Economic Crisis. Was it Influenced by the Crisis?',*Proceedings of the 13th International Symposium in Management: Management During and After the Economic Crisis*, 9-10 October, Timisoara. Amsterdam: Elsevier, pp.317-325.

Zhao, S., Yu, H. & Liu, Z. (2011) 'An Empirical Study of the Theoretical Model between Higher Education Input and Economic Growth', *China Higher Education Research*, 9, pp.11-15.

Zhong, H. (2012) 'Comparisons of Problems in the Innovation System of the BRICS', *Science & Technology Progress and Policy*, 29(2), pp.1-5.

Zhu, H. & Lou S. (2011) *Development and Reform of Higher Education in China*. Cambridge: Woodhead Publishing Limited.

9. Appendix

Presented below are the tables of the log-transformed country specific GDP plus the enrolled population in tertiary academic degree programs as well as the enrolled students in tertiary vocational training institutions in each BRICS country over the research period of 21 years starting from 1994 and ending in 2014.

a. Russian data   b. Brazilian data

RUSSIA	LGDP	LEDU	LVOE	BRAZIL	LGDP	LEDU	LVOE
1994	2.96	2.66	2.12	1994	3.12	2.23	2.61
1995	2.94	2.65	2.15	1995	3.14	2.25	2.56
1996	2.93	2.67	2.17	1996	3.15	2.27	2.50
1997	2.93	2.69	2.20	1997	3.17	2.31	2.43
1998	2.91	2.72	2.20	1998	3.17	2.34	2.35
1999	2.94	2.76	2.22	1999	3.17	2.39	2.26
2000	2.98	2.80	2.24	2000	3.19	2.44	2.14
2001	3.00	2.86	2.26	2001	3.19	2.49	1.96
2002	3.02	2.90	2.28	2002	3.21	2.55	1.67
2003	3.05	2.93	2.30	2003	3.21	2.60	1.66
2004	3.08	2.93	2.31	2004	3.24	2.63	1.86
2005	3.11	2.95	2.31	2005	3.25	2.66	1.88
2006	3.14	2.96	2.29	2006	3.27	2.69	1.94
2007	3.18	2.97	2.27	2007	3.29	2.72	2.00
2008	3.20	2.98	2.22	2008	3.31	2.78	2.05
2009	3.16	2.97	2.19	2009	3.31	2.79	2.09
2010	3.18	2.95	2.19	2010	3.34	2.82	2.12
2011	3.20	2.94	2.19	2011	3.36	2.84	2.15
2012	3.22	2.90	2.20	2012	3.37	2.86	2.18
2013	3.22	2.88	2.19	2013	3.38	2.88	1.94
2014	3.22	2.84	2.17	2014	3.38	2.91	1.95

c. Indian data   d. Chinese data

INDIA	LGDP	LEDU	LVOE	CHINA	LGDP	LEDU	LVOE
1994	2.75	2.69	1.93	1994	3.12	2.65	2.91
1995	2.78	2.69	1.89	1995	3.17	2.72	2.96
1996	2.81	2.76	1.86	1996	3.21	2.75	3.00
1997	2.83	2.78	1.89	1997	3.25	2.77	3.04
1998	2.86	2.86	1.82	1998	3.28	2.78	3.07
1999	2.89	2.92	1.75	1999	3.31	2.80	3.11
2000	2.91	2.97	1.79	2000	3.35	2.87	3.09
2001	2.93	2.99	1.71	2001	3.38	2.97	3.08
2002	2.95	3.02	1.79	2002	3.42	3.08	3.07
2003	2.98	3.05	1.85	2003	3.46	3.18	3.05
2004	3.01	3.07	1.87	2004	3.51	3.26	3.10
2005	3.05	3.07	1.87	2005	3.55	3.31	3.15
2006	3.09	3.11	1.87	2006	3.60	3.37	3.18
2007	3.12	3.17	1.87	2007	3.66	3.40	3.24
2008	3.14	3.24	1.92	2008	3.70	3.43	3.28
2009	3.18	3.27	1.98	2009	3.74	3.47	3.30
2010	3.22	3.32	2.04	2010	3.79	3.49	3.31
2011	3.25	3.43	2.09	2011	3.82	3.50	3.31
2012	3.27	3.46	2.14	2012	3.86	3.51	3.29
2013	3.30	3.45	2.18	2013	3.89	3.53	3.33
2014	3.33	3.48	2.20	2014	3.92	3.62	3.28

e. South African data

SOUTH AFRICA	LGDP	LEDU	LVOE
1994	2.35	1.79	0.68
1995	2.37	1.81	0.88
1996	2.39	1.82	1.02
1997	2.40	1.83	1.12
1998	2.40	1.85	1.21
1999	2.41	1.86	1.21
2000	2.43	1.87	1.30
2001	2.44	1.89	1.34
2002	2.45	1.90	1.39
2003	2.47	1.91	1.41
2004	2.49	1.92	1.44
2005	2.51	1.93	1.36
2006	2.53	1.94	1.39
2007	2.55	1.95	1.43
2008	2.57	1.96	1.43
2009	2.56	1.97	1.43
2010	2.57	1.98	1.34
2011	2.59	1.99	1.35
2012	2.60	2.00	1.39
2013	2.61	2.02	1.43
2014	2.61	2.01	1.47

Druck:
Canon Deutschland Business Services GmbH
im Auftrag der KNV-Gruppe
Ferdinand-Jühlke-Str. 7
99095 Erfurt